# A BOY ASLEEP

# A BOY ASLEEP UNDER THE SUN

*Versions of Sandro Penna*
*by Peter Valente*

punctum books ✳ brooklyn, ny

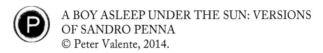

A BOY ASLEEP UNDER THE SUN: VERSIONS
OF SANDRO PENNA
© Peter Valente, 2014.

First published in 2014 by
punctum books
Brooklyn, New York
http://punctumbooks.com

ISBN-13: 978-0692296936
ISBN-10: 069229693X

Cover Image: Jean-Jacques Henner, *A Young Bather Asleep*, 1982. Unterlinden Museum, Colmar, France.

Before you start to read this book, take this moment to think about making a donation to punctum books, an independent non-profit press,

@ http://punctumbooks.com/about/

If you're reading the e-book, you can click on the image below to go directly to our donations site. Any amount, no matter the size, is appreciated and will help us to keep our ship of fools afloat. Contributions from dedicated readers will also help us to keep our commons open and to cultivate new work that can't find a welcoming port elsewhere. Our ad/venture is not possible without your support. Vive la open-access.

*Fig.* 1. Hieronymous Bosch, *Ship of Fools* (1490-1500)

# CONTENTS

## FOREWORD

My first encounter with Sandro Penna's poetry was while translating Pier Paolo Pasolini. At the time I was reading a biography on Pasolini and learned of his close friendship with Penna. Pasolini insisted that among serious readers of poetry Penna could not be ignored. There I learned Penna was by profession an accountant but literature was always more important to him. He read Leopardi, Hölderlin, Rimbaud, Baudelaire and Crevel. Later he worked briefly as a translator, translating Paul Claudel and Prosper Mérimée. He wrote occasionally for newspapers but wrote almost only poetry. He also worked as a proofreader and art dealer but he never held a regular job, preferring to remain anonymous. He enjoyed long walks in fields, parks, and working-class neighborhoods, often at night. He entered the world of letters through the intervention of Umberto Saba, who along with Cesare Pavese and Eugenio Montale, helped secure the publication of his first poems in the early 30s. In a video of Penna reading his poems I saw a charming elderly man seated on the edge of a bed with a thin book open before him, in a cramped and disorderly room. His voice retained something of a childlike tone yet it was firm and clear. There was no artifice. The poems were read as though they were responses in a conversation, quickly, almost casually and unassumingly. Penna smiled when reading a certain poem (I later discovered it was a poem for Rafaelle that I will speak about in a moment) recalling an experience of joy. These poems were part of a lived experience.

Penna himself believed his best poems were his shortest,

those of two, three, or four lines. Penna is a poet of the present moment. In this age when we are bombarded by images that move so fast we can't possibly process them all, Penna's poetry seems like a radical gesture indeed. In a sense, Penna's poetry is closer to photography or painting. Perhaps this is one reason why his poetry is so unlike most twentieth-century Italian poetry. The poems are like spontaneous brushstrokes that capture, in the manner of an impressionist painter, the sensation of a moment already past. But this memory emerges in the present, vividly, in the stroke of the brush, in the poem:

> It is deserted down by the riverbank. And you know it's
>     enough
> after the solar braveries of last night.
> I kissed your armpits, a damp, fierce pleasure. The odor
>     reminds me
> of that failed summer long ago.

The word "solar" is a central word for Penna. On the one hand, it refers to daylight as opposed to night, "the color of dawn" and "the black of night". But the word also describes the nature of an event, an action (i.e. homosexual sex). It is "brave" because it is outside the law. "Solar" refers to Apollo, the god of the sun who is associated with males, clarity, celibacy and/or homosexuality. It is important to note here that Apollo and Dionysus, the dark chthonic god associated with females and thus with the moon, are not opposing forces in Penna's poetry. The Dionysian also refers to unconstrained sex and there is a hedonistic quality to the poems. But there is a complex relation between the lunar, the world of darkness and the ancient love (i.e. homosexuality, particularly Greek paiderastēs). The dark of night is Penna's "color / It is the splendor of absolute darkness". In the poem "To the Moon", this darkness is associated with visibility: "How clear to you is this face I keep hidden". But in the following poem there is a conflict between his "ancient" love and the "sweet laughing moon":

It was a happy May evening. And you, sweet moon,
perhaps you laugh at the loves of the ancients.
And so I must leave you, O sweet laughing moon,
O my ancient moon.

In another poem the tension is between this "ancient love" imagined as a fire "in the silence of the night" and the "fierce winds" that seek to quench it:

Oh this rank lamentation
born of a remorse so ancient.
It is a fire in the silence of night
under fierce winds.

There is a tension in Penna's poetry between darkness and light, disclosure and anonymity, that is never fully resolved since they are not opposed forces but superimposed states, the discontinuous but always latent behavior of the libido. Penna rarely speaks of history. Yet here in three lines he evokes years of suffering which recall to the reader the atrocities of World War II:

To the first murmur of autumn

the cheerful Allied train speaks
of unimaginable distance and horror.

He is direct and speaks strictly about what moves him. His lyrics on the love of young boys are as candid as the poems of Catullus:

You will die my sweet little boy and so will I.
Nothing is more beautiful than watching you asleep
on the seashore under a bright sun.

Not yet, O no not yet.

His poems are not complicated by the excessive metaphor that characterized the Hermetic school of Italian poetry in the 30s. One of his early influences was Eugenio Montale whom he first met along with Saba in 1932. Though their poetry is very different, Penna dedicated his last published poem to Montale:

*To Eugenio Montale*

I walk toward the festivals at dusk,
opposite the crowd who happily and quickly
rise from the stadium seats to cheer.
I don't look at anyone but I see everyone.
Sometimes I pick up a smile.
More rarely a familiar regard.

But I no longer remember who they are.
I know death solves nothing.

It is too unfair.
Even if I no longer remember who they are.

His poems reminded me of the early work of the American poet John Wieners. In Penna's poetry there is that same quality of sustenance when faced with deprivation. Desire finds strength in resignation: "Love's punishment is not worth listening to anymore. / It won't heal the wound."

In Penna's poetry ecstasy and despair are dependent on the presence or absence of the gods of love:

Oh how I want to kiss the boy.
Sun aligns with moon, forests underneath the sea.
Everyone at the same time kissing a mouth.

But the child does not know it. He runs to the door
above which hangs a sad light.
And his mouth is numb like the dead.

There is pleasure when the gods are present and when there is no interference from the ego. Eros is activated. The "I" feels larger than life because sexuality acts as a drug:

*EROTIC*

This body that I pull towards me
and which clenches me in return
has the taste of mud mixed with starlight.
And I don't know who stains me now.
It's a mysterious game

when the tincture of the stars
turns a deep red.

For Penna, "the pleasure / of abandonment / obeys no grammar / but its own". But there is an alternate state, the collapse into the literal, the end of pleasure and a consequent denial of the gods. Anguish is present; the gods of love have fled:

I, seated on a bench in the darkness, alone, empty,
was once Hölderlin…Rimbaud…

Anger is directed toward the ego:

Now, without allies
I reequip myself for a new war.
It is against myself.
And here I am very efficient.

Like Wieners, Penna was persuaded and deluded enough to be a poet in love with the world. This love oscillates between an ecstatic feeling of selflessness and the return to a former unhappiness. But, finally, the poet is blind before the mysteries of life. For Penna, life does not reveal the mystery of self:

But what is the truth of my life?
    I don't know.
And the rising sun doesn't say

I read that Penna was the first person Pasolini sought out

when he arrived in Rome in 1950. Born in Perugia on June 12, 1906, Penna lived most of his life in Rome (he died there on January 21, 1977) except for a brief period in Milan where he worked as a library clerk. Thus Pasolini trusted Penna to "show him around". He knew that Penna was in love with the same ragazzi who prowled the outskirts of Rome. Pasolini told a reporter that since Montale was already considered a great poet the Nobel Prize should be given to Penna. He knew that Penna would be "destined to be a poet at the margins, not known, even despised, whereas in fact he is a very great poet."

In his poetry Penna clearly said who he was and how he felt. He spoke of what he wanted. And that is a rare enough quality these days. Thus Penna moves away from the trappings of identity toward an honest expression of love. In Penna's work the beautiful is not conscious of itself and is therefore erotic: "Is not the beauty of those who are unaware of their beauty / more beautiful than those who are aware?" He is critical of those who hide their desires behind a thin façade of modesty:

Here they are, these lords of life.
They are very modest, indeed.
Even with their senses fully aroused,
they manage to offend no one.

Or behind the vagaries of personal style:

Your righteous arrogance
in regard to my nasty gesture
seemed strangely gentle

gilded, of course, by your personal style.

He can be as sharp as Pasolini in his assessment of a "superior" temperament:

Oh don't put on
superior airs. Once
I saw a look worthy of that.
It was when a baby was annoyed
at a party.

Or as disgusted with consumer culture:

Today even beauty can be bought and sold,
purchased like any common object,
without feeling and without any high-minded ideals.
Today, anything goes.

He has an instinct for the lyrical and is a master of the epigram. The following is as close as Penna ever came to stating a "poetics":

The drizzle outside doesn't bore me.
Instead, I am inspired to write this.
Whoever doesn't trust in this sudden rush of emotion
will speak falsely when he speaks.

Penna never hid his sexuality in interviews. He once told a reporter (who probably had to pay dearly for the interview), "I am not a homosexual. I am a pederasta… Homosexuality is a privilege." Penna's homosexuality is complicated in one sense by a moral dilemma:

> The problem of sex
> consumes my entire life.
> I wonder at each moment
> whether I am doing the right thing
> or the wrong.

But there is another sense in which Penna accepts the impossibility of a moral resolution to his "problem" and instead turns this negative to a positive value:

> There are always boys in my poems.
> But I do not know how to speak of anything else.
> Everything else is just a tedious noise.
> I am unable to sing of Good Deeds.

In 1956 he brought a 14 year old street kid, Rafaelle Cedrino, to the home he shared with his mother and stayed with him on and off for fourteen years. Penna wrote this epigram for the young boy:

> I saw my dark haired boy
> seated in the audience
> smoking a cigarette
> he has the brightest eyes

Since his poems chiefly concern homosexual love they face being relegated to a gay-only ghetto of readers or to another ghetto that even homosexuals avoid: pederastia. This is a problematic issue in the United States where scandal surrounding sexual orientation is still prevalent. But more importantly, there are no glamorous pronouncements or concern with gender politics in Penna's poetry. You also won't find a vision of historical process or a mass of physical details. What you will find is an attachment to everyday reality. Penna's poetry is candid, uncluttered, minimalist, and of profound lyrical intensity and as Pasolini, a great supporter of Penna's work, wrote in the 1970 preface to Penna's collected poems, he is, "perhaps the greatest and most joyful… Italian poet."

## A NOTE ON THE TRANSLATION

The following are not literal translations. These poems emerged from an intense and sustained conversation with Penna's poetry. They are "free" renditions or variations and form my own personal portrait of Sandro Penna.

There is nothing I can do
but go on led by the flickering of a flame
I cannot name.

-John Wieners

**POEMS**
*(1927-1955)*

The air of Spring
invades the city.
The boys of the night
grow a little older.

Every punishment has fallen upon me. Now
it rains quietly on my life.
In the distance I see a young mechanic
in his garage working on a motor.

I close the book I was reading,
and embark for that distant life.
But what is the truth of my life?
            I don't know.
And the rising sun doesn't say.

The dull crowd wanders around the music hall,
happy and unaware of the things that surround them.
The solitary beauty waits…

She is invisible to everyone,
but most of all to herself

Even if the wind
muffles the sounds of Spring,
the songs of the people can be heard
throughout the night.

I listen to them while lying in bed. I put down
"The Life of Jesus." The songs excite me
and I burn when I hear their voices.

When midnight comes the men are still
attached to their drinks and their newfound companions.
But suddenly they remember the dreams of youth,
and by a stroke of grace, they finally see
slowly unfolding before them,
in the drunken haze, an adolescent face.
They are then reminded of their own broken dreams.

Sadness doesn't live
along the streets of the old suburb.
These boys dressed in rags
live a gentle life,
gilded by the sun
That's enough.

If my boy appears at a hotel,
the men, amazed, smile at him
from under the neon lights. But the game begins
almost immediately. Uncertain and alone,
the boy is in the grip
of these big hands adorned with rings.

Pleasant days come and go. So too,
the pleasures of a beautiful age are no longer.
What remains are these prohibitions
to our happiness.

Outside in the rain you search for him.
You look everywhere for a sign. You lose patience.
But then it returns, leading you on.  You
ignore the rain, you are on fire. The rain
falls harder. But the doors, these
doors of the world are locked. You are not welcome.
Seek shelter somewhere else,
and turn off your light.

My poetry is not some lightweight game
with sensitive words
or sick
(Clear March sun
on the shivering leaves of a plane tree,
too green in the light.)
My poetry will launch its vertical force
and lose itself in the infinite
(Games of a handsome athlete
during the lengthy summer evenings.)

The world that seems to you made of chains
is in fact a vast mosaic of profound harmonies.

There are always boys in my poems.
But I do not know how to speak of anything else.
Everything is just a tedious noise.
I am unable to sing of Good Deeds.

Oh this rank lamentation
born of a remorse so ancient.
It is a fire in the silence of night
under fierce winds.

Like a fly
trapped in honey…

## THE TOMB OF MY FATHER

I stand here in the eastern part of the cemetery
where he is buried. The sun hides
behind a mass of clouds.
A young boy detaches himself from his mother
and pisses in the direction of the soldiers. It is desolate
out here in the countryside. He laughs but I can sense
that there is a sadness in his heart.

My little boy is like the April wind,
clear and light, and somewhat mutable.
The grass is so warm and there is a fresh breeze. Yet,
it is vain to think there is constancy in its caress.

The trains that languished on the tracks once,
are silent and unmoving now. Oh my foolish life
with it's persistent hunger. Now, alone
and anxious, you work the streets at night
with that stubborn cough that won't let up,
in the last cold days of February.

It is deserted down by the riverbank. And you know it's enough
after the solar braveries of last night.
I kissed your armpits, a damp, fierce pleasure. The odor reminds me
of that failed summer long ago.

If the sweet honey-colored wind returns,
these young lascivious animals will abandon
the hallowed steps of the church.

You don't love the walls of this room.
In your eyes there is a red flower
that seeks escape. You think
of the young acrobat, of his triumph,
of your own life when the Spring returns.

In the garden, one day, I saw the boys blushing.
They have nothing. And yet they were sure of themselves.
They already smiled back at life.

My life is monotonous. A quiet sun
burns on the green shutters.
It looks with docile eyes. It is a calm anonymous love,
in the poetry of these four lines.

A simple poetry descends
upon the distracted traveller, takes hold of him
in the station, among the dreary crowds,
his hand on the shoulder of a boy.

A little boy raced behind a train.
Live, he shouted to me, without restraint.
I motioned to him with my hand, laughing.
I was startled by his boldness
and yet calmly I stood there in a daze
while the train sped past me into the distant haze.

Together with their parents these beautiful boys
will climb toward the highest peak. I see
the embarrassed look in their eyes.
But we remain here below. We are not sad
but poor, hungry soldiers.

The light with which I burn is a private flame.
When the sun is lustful and the stunned boys
follow my call, I can hear the tinkling of crowns
announce a new baptism.

The insomnia of the swallows. A dear friend
salutes me at the train station, 3 am in the morning.

The accused has nothing if not the right words.
And sometimes there are none, sometimes
he would prefer not to speak at all.
The only true words are born of solar need.

Perhaps I'll age faster if I continue to take these long trips,
always seated for hours, with nothing to see outside but the
    rain,
nothing but a tired ray of light that falls on a life of
    silence....
(The workers seized what they could and left the train.
They came from the suburbs to a sweet lake, and brought
    back
only their exhausted bodies and their utensils).
When I climbed into bed next to them I shouted,
We are just men and tired, we are not sick or cowardly as
    you make us out to be.

Someone had come to disturb your heart.
He was one of those spectators who are free and without a
    name,
assorted types who are indifferent in their boredom.
And you suddenly feel joy in the winter.

Someone had come but your heart is tired. You feel old.
He was one of those adolescents who are free and without
    love,
assorted types who are indifferent in their joy.
And you are bored with the drama of their sins.

Someone had come and then went away,
leaving you like a fruit in a basket,
for sale on the market.

Like a wave surging to the edge of the rock-cliff
so is my desire for him.
It is love.
But he doesn't know how much,
not the heights of joy nor the abyss of tears.

I loved everything in the world. And I possessed nothing but my golden book of words.

O bright cemetery light, do not tell me
that the summer night isn't beautiful.
The drinkers inside those distant inns are beautiful.

They move like friezes
across the night sky with stars.

O bright cemetery light, calmly you say
their days and nights are numbered. No, don't tell me
the summer night isn't beautiful.

To sit at an unfamiliar table.
To sleep in a foreign bed.
To feel the emptiness of the deserted piazza.
To feel your throat tighten and your eyes swell
as you tenderly wave goodbye.

This was my city, this city of vacant dawns. I know it well.
I walk its streets at all hours. In any weather.
It is full of my desires.
My poems of love are my truth yet they
remain unknown among all the other poems
that proclaim the fashions of the day.

# NOTES
*(1938-1949)*

Happy are those who are different
in private.
But woe to those who are different
in public.

A dream of beauty in which he seized me.
I was aflame in an otherwise warm country.

When the world's manifold forms
strike a luminous glow near the nimble sun of October,
both cruel and happy is my dream of pleasure.

Then he turned his face toward my cheek,
and smiled to himself O blessed scarlet
his face lit up.

And after, I was alone in bed,
and for sweet company
the memory of his bold yet innocent lies.

Oh, Zelinda, my thoughts no longer know your nights.
While dreaming perhaps you enjoy again the many pastries.
    Or perhaps
you are laughing, shedding tears again while watching the
    clowns
in the variety show.

I saw a yellow and green colored cart.
The streets were covered with snow and the sea was a cold
    blue.
I forgot the world outside: the mud and the sun, too,
seemed useless and a sickly yellow. But then I saw
a group of adolescent boys at play
under that same yellow sun. I hid
behind the yellow and green cart,
and watched them walk down the street
until they turned the corner and vanished.

Perhaps you can lose this lingering sadness
if you entrust your life
to a speeding train at night.

Then it became a poor thing, dejected,
held in your hand, secretly,
the sign of your life.

It is the noble sex. And so, after years in the life
you find yourself older (noble, yes, but still young at heart!).
These are rare specimens of men.
Finally, ....you appear, again and again,
a single image so dear to me.

Is not the construction of it a happy gift
from nature. Others call it a flower.

Whimsical childish ineptitude
latches onto me, uncertain. But what is certain
is that time will pass
despite these delinquent pleasures of the seed.

You don't want me. You speak of "natural" beauty,
the kind that women know and cherish. After all,
your vanity pleases them.

Is not the timidity you hide behind a stern façade,
perhaps your confused dream of God?

You are a beautiful youth. Stop for a moment,
drink a little wine and then you'll see what they can do.
Yes, at first the boys are a little rough.

I was born among you. Yet I am not of you. I knew
the normal family life: father mother hence a brother
a quiet sister without makeup.
But already a wolf cub with the eyes of a lamb…

The victory was wild and sweet
don't you see? If everybody whistles and shouts the result
you'll have to give up, resigned to your empty salute.

My heart overflows in the damp silent night.
Smoke rises from the pipes.
Goodbye cold vigor of youth. I won't miss your sad walls.

They are alone and tied up but comfortable. They're
    married.
Outside in the night: the freedom of the roaring winter
    wind.

Ah, in the dead of night
the dog barks. But in the morning,
the dog is lonely
and he licks your hand.

The lucent shoulders
wrestle in the swimming pool.
Select men dare.

On the farm
warm shade
is common. And men.

Here is the beloved city and you say the oppressive night
does not alarm you. Solitary friends pass by
and look at you. They wink and give you looks of love.
Or so you think…

# THE STRANGE JOY OF LIVING
*(1949-1955)*

The tenderness the tenderness is revealed
when new things about tenderness are named.

Oh don't put on
superior airs. Once
I saw a look worthy of that.
It was when a baby was annoyed
at a party.

Your righteous arrogance
in regard to my nasty gesture
seemed strangely gentle
gilded, of course, by your personal style.

How beautiful it is to follow a youth
while the city sleeps at night. You hesitate.
If you suddenly stop at the corner,
and remain there at a distance,
I will stay where I am, far from you
and leave you at peace. Oh my solitude
is like a flickering candle in the wind.

Lonely, you stand near the fountain,
your face reflected in the water.
The raw poetry of the military decoration
burns in your heart with a fire
greater than Botticelli's Venus.

The stars looked at me and it was as if a ray of light opened halfway like the slit of a cat's eye.

Your life is pleasing and gentle.
Along the way appeared a well-dressed gentleman,
full of love but who was, simply, a worm.
Your life is quiet and unconcerned with style.

The cyclist with the dirty face
can only offer the bride
his vow of celibacy.

Walking over a bridge at twilight
I gaze at the horizon.
You seem to vanish from my mind.

But the countryside remains
full of the novel reality of things.
All these useless blue balloons
not worth a second thought.

I lay between two young wiseasses
who mocked the words of my heart.
As I gaze at their sleeping faces,
I forgive them with love.

The skinny boy returns home
a little tired but very interested
in those things that concern the bus. He thinks
—with that light that comes from the senses
that light that still barely touches-
about all the possible ways
to use something new. Something
that won't take hold,
though sometimes he touches it.
Then he notices me. Now he feels cold.
He blows on his heart
which he holds in his big hands.

I have to get off and it's probably just as well.

In all my romances
I didn't only love the outer form,
but also the fragile sweetness that is lost
between these mountains of strength.

**SACRED AND PROFANE**
*(1927-1957)*

What do you want with a boy in this world.
Even the dogs circle around you and bark loudly.

Oh happy life where I expose
each of my sweet solitary madnesses.

It's great to work in a darkened room
with my head on vacation
somewhere along the waves of the blue sea.

Boys, from this June night,
don't come back here anymore.
I think you know why.
But as I said and as I say to you now,
you must go
this evening,
whoever you are.

Even if the other girls…
Oh just ignore them.
But I know you are not
truly cured of them.
Wander a bit,
go on a little trip
together (like twins?).
There embrace them
and pretend.
That which is true
will come out one day.

By what stroke of grace am I able to separate
bright sun from turgid waters.

You will recover.
You hear the distant trains—the city at night
and the peal of the North wind.
After a day's hard work you fell asleep for an instant
waiting for the sounds of the chimes
to bring you back to that forgotten place.

Love, youth, why do these sweet words
make you shine but also shrivel?
An odor of dried manure remains
along the row of hedges drenched with sun.

.

We live to love someone.
Today it is this boy who has stolen a pair of shoes
from an arrogant Signore.

I defended him and I saved him
from who knows what dark retribution.
He is one of those Southern boys
who steal handsome dogs in order to love them.

Alone in the night looking at the stars,
I listened to a youth speak about his life
and what I heard were the vital words
of a new dialect.

**ODDITIES**
*(1957-1976)*

# 1
*(1957-1965)*

## TO THE MOON

How clear to you is this face I keep hidden.
I stand under the shade of the Grand Hotel.
I am shielded from view but left with my private chaos.
    Either
happiness or pain, or perhaps the shadow of a poor dog in
    an alleyway
or a little boy that stays the night, only these things can ease
my discontent. I don't want
these animals that howl in the street at night.

Perhaps the secret story of my extreme passion
was born on the green grass of a suburban town
or on vacation somewhere.
It is rain pouring down from silent swollen clouds.
Bright lights of the city      the empty countryside.

You will die my sweet little boy and so will I.
Nothing is more beautiful than watching you asleep
on the seashore under a bright sun.


Not yet, O no not yet.

Last summer you kissed me on the mouth.
Now please say to me you won't go so far away.
Please return with your love firmly intact,
and don't be so concerned about your weight.
Vanity is so unattractive.

The drizzle outside doesn't bore me.
Instead, I am inspired to write this.
Whoever doesn't trust in this sudden rush of emotion
will speak falsely when he speaks.

The fool is like an accordion of pain.
He is idle but confident at work,
building up a sweat that drenches his white collar.

It happened at the cinema,
near the exit to the toilets,
where the doors open
and close, continuously. She thinks,
listening to the creaking sound,
that it's her husband,
who left a few minutes ago.
She passes the time,
anxiously.

But he doesn't return.

Perhaps inspiration is only a confused cry.
These young boys laugh at the dictates of the Law
as they jerk him off in the toilet.

Midsummer at night.
You close your windows and bar the door
to satisfy your desire for a comfortable, familiar life.
My silence hides,
seething in the dark foliage below.

The love of the two sexes
adds to the comedy.

WEEPING

From a grand tenement,
full of bright electric lights I hear the noise
of tin cans and running water.
It is an absurd and useless sound. A
child is crying somewhere.
But childhood, if I remember
can be somewhat disorderly and desperate.

OF NO USE

Under the lights your weak laughter
is useless. Close the shutters, pay attention
with your eyes. Look at me. And yet I can't help
laughing. You're afraid. Why?
Just open the shutters.
Your desire has left you confused.

This great love lasted only a week.
Ah, and yet the longer love lasts
the more time there is for error.

EROTIC

This body that I pull towards me
and which clenches me in return
has the taste of mud mixed with starlight.
And I don't know whose stains me now.
It's a mysterious game
when the tincture of the stars
turns a deep red.

Even if you feel shy and confused,
this dark room is a paradise for your senses
my dear boy. No, not those absurd places
where they dance among the false glittering lights.
Here, your virgin lust can freely sing.

To the first murmur of autumn
the cheerful Allied train speaks
of unimaginable distance and horror.

When I greeted you in the old days
they used to wave their handkerchiefs.
Everything was a ritual, then.

Today a boy
puts two fingers in his mouth.
The world must interpret the sign
and only then do they run kneeling before an altar.

It was a happy May evening. And you, sweet moon,
perhaps you laugh at the loves of the ancients.
And so I must leave you, O sweet laughing moon,
O my ancient moon.

You say, "escape," but why doesn't
the poor shepherd on the hill feel this need?
The fountains of St. Peter's shine. Where
can you escape to? The Coliseum
is dangerous among the ruins.

Although the sun's motion
is apparent and precise,
it seemed now was the time
for its revolution to cease,
eternally.

He looked at the Gothic façade.
He listened in the night
and heard the rare sound of footsteps.
Then you hid behind a column.
Loving guardian, the promise of your treasure
is broken when there is silence.

A sweet gift
this life
where the pleasure
of abandonment
obeys no grammar
but its own.

Oh sad fact of my life
that my secret muse, my own desire, was at first
a little praised by the critics.
Perhaps I have loved too much
since now they only curse my words.

Were these acts of love only despised
because they could no longer be comprehended?

The bicycle in the bright sun awaits
the unkempt child who is without a voice in society.

How gentle and beautiful were these signs of life,
the men flourishing in the midst of the crowded piazza.
But for some reason they are still considered mad
and useless to life.

My intimate concessions
disrupt the critic's discourse.

They have called me
"The exclusive poet of love."
And perhaps this is true.
But the wind here that blows
on each blade of grass
and the noises of the distant city
whose lights are visible from where I stand,
do they not also speak of love?
And are there not behind these warm clouds
the sounds of an ardent love beyond which
there is nothing but silence?

The air darkens as the day
slowly closes around him.

But the voices of birds can be heard
on the damp riverbank. On the street
festive crowds gather for the night
and the secret signal can be heard
in the whistle of the bicyclists.

The invisible trains
hidden behind the gilded smoke and the urgent appeals
will carry us to an unknown destination.
We won't be melancholy like him tonight.

The problem of sex
consumes my entire life.
I wonder at each moment
whether I am doing the right thing
or the wrong.

Oh how I want to kiss the beautiful boy.
Sun aligns with moon, the forests underneath the sea.
Everyone at the same time kissing a mouth.

But the child does not know it. He runs to the door
above which hangs a sad light.
And his mouth is numb like the dead.

Virility laughs. It is both fierce and gentle to Rome, yet it laughs and scintillates with a secret energy.

Everyone has a touch of vulgarity these days,
even those who are embarrassed or confused.
That one there who calms my desires,
is uncertain of his own.

The storm has ended
and the calm air returns.
Unmoved, I remain in bed all day long
drunk with this state of serene melancholy.

The pleasing sound of the bells.
The pleasing smoke of the minestra.
The happy house in the bright sun.
O love, my love, where is the gypsy in you?

I ride a horse down to the riverbank
but when a thought enters my head
and I begin to think,
the horse slowly comes to a halt. Strange.

The autumn wind ruffles the blinds.
I see the rebellious youth who salutes me.
His eyes are firm and luminous
there, behind the blinds. Looking at me.

**2**

*(1965-1970)*

Black fire foaming in the sea.
Your eyes, a confused dream
of trains and loneliness. O my love,
I watch you all night long.

Good and evil coexist in the lure of your gaze.

A room with patio furniture in a small village near Rome.
The bell tower above the empty bed.
Is love perhaps the tight rope we walk
between despair and a vision of the beloved?

Here they are, these lords of life.
They are very modest, indeed.
Even with their senses fully aroused,
they manage to offend no one.

The young boy's eyes are the color of dawn
and the bright lights of early evening sparkle
like a perverse young girl.
But the black of night is my color.
It is the splendor of absolute darkness.

I was seated as the streetcar door closed.
From a small window I watch the delicious fog cloak the
	towns
as they speed past.
But then, a mysterious sadness interrupts my joy.

How much sadness is there for these happy young people
who are bred in the comforts of life?

Oh this lukewarm peace where time stands still.
But in my heart, there is a light that never goes out.
It is the sun that glazes the blades of grass.

Oh this lukewarm peace. A secret lust
is born, I now know, from the first light of dawn.

FROM RIMBAUD

…then the wild ones will rise bringing with them new and
     glorious battalions.
In the evening they will sing new songs of magic and
     science until the voice is hoarse.
They will frighten the hearts of these honorable gentlemen.

You are waiting for someone in the park. Your rose-colored
    cheeks
display a false innocence
and there is the sinister rustle of your black dress.
You disturb the destiny of these green boys on park benches
in the sun of a quiet Sunday afternoon.

He turned slightly to the left. No, this was a trick of vision.
But he did remember the years that still seemed like
    yesterday
when he raced like a madman between boredom and a
    vision of the beloved.
He remembers the time when tight shorts were all the rage.

FROM VERLAINE (BEAMS)

I disgust him. He is restless and gentle,
a bit vulgar perhaps.
No, do not believe it is safe for a minute.

To be the preferred ones
they must see us now as proud and fierce

so suppress these thoughts
and take him back from the lonesome road.
He is yours.

The pine trees have absorbed the lazy joy of the changing seasons for a long time, regardless of lovers who come and go or the human cycle of birth and death.

I submitted to the delicacy of his hands.
Outside, the wind brushed against the homes of adults.
To the left you can see the slow migration of children.

I look up at the sky
and ask myself:
what do I expect,
what do I crave?
Everything is peaceful
but for this veil
of sadness O
do not
ask.

My life is completely burned out.
Yet I live happily in my dissolution.
Love's punishment is not worth listening to anymore.
It won't heal the wound.

Their secret cravings, their wild victories
are all kept confidential.
(during the summer they squandered
whole days,
wandering together in foreign cities at night.)
When tired, they slept
in each other's arms.
Their naked bodies greet the dawn.
This is an entirely natural desire.

Is it time
to resume my wanderings?
O dear and ardent sea
I come to you now.

It is time. Perhaps to adjourn.
I do not know.
Here, take me. With my drunken anguish
and this rush of joy that overwhelms me.

My father is dead.
He was not old when he died
and yet he was called to that unknown journey
too soon.
He was like an old friend
from the time I was a child,
when I first discovered in him
a companion of the evening,
home from work.

Now, as the light grows dim
among the trees, under the stars,
I listen to life. It appears to move slower
with an inexplicable melancholy. Yet it was the same
those evenings long ago lit up again in memory.
The same recurs in these beautiful children.

Of all the shy young men
you are by far the worst.

Oh beautiful dream of athletes on the playing field.
Oh sweet reality I know so well.

**3**
*(1970-1976)*

It rained on our ardent love
all summer long. Then the color changed:
a beautiful sun-soaked countryside appeared.

There is no longer that lightening grace
but the murmur of something that is to come.

Once, I conducted a loving yet merciless war
against these young boys. Now, without allies
I reequip myself for a new war.
It is against myself.
And here I am very efficient.

When I returned home I saw a river of blood
streaming from the hands of the crucified.
It seemed to mock my clothes and the dirt on my face.

These days, I don't go home anymore.
Filth has infected the soul.
And now it was my turn to laugh.

Over there, under the bright sun
the personal history of the dead is written.
Higher above, it seemed to me,
there was a clearing
where bones were left as a reminder.
Today a cow with no sense of history sniffs
the black earth still fuming. Enclosed between
the filaments of rain, there are sparse but certain
threads of memory.

Across the river, during an evening in July,
I hear the song of drunken boys at play.
I, seated on a bench in the darkness, alone, empty,
was once Hölderlin… Rimbaud…

Here the sun seems so warm
and the flowers ardently bloom in bucketfuls.
And here words are only sounds without meaning.
Oh foreigner you are happy wherever you are.

Is not the beauty of those who are unaware of their beauty more beautiful than those who are aware?

I move toward the sun,
careful with my zipper.

Oh the tiresome neverending complaints of these nuns
who are crazier than those inside the convent,
with their empty protests that ring like a bell
above the silent rooftops of this mad city
in the cold windy night.

Today even beauty can be bought and sold,
purchased like any common object,
without feeling and without any high-minded ideals.
Today, anything goes.

You know how difficult it is to love you
and also love what the supreme craftsman says
on his silent altar.

Your moods are of the earth.
With a single finger you can erase
the cold of myth, the void
he left when he vanished.

Red in the face and raging my enemy draws near:
It smells like mamma. Something unknown stirs in me at
    the sight.
I am surprised after all this time: the bottle
is my friend again. Meanwhile my enemy,
having defeated and humiliated me twice before in battle,
is giddy with happiness.

My final book is dedicated
to those who were my first loves.
Out of sheer idleness, I have not thanked them enough
or given them news about myself.

# THE SLEEPLESS TRAVELLER
*(1977)*

At the sound of the first cricket
when there is still light,
I denounced the long barren list of dinner invitations.

Through the black cloud of coal dust,
he greets me with a radiant smile.
But the wooden angel on the masthead
guards the sad and fragrant urinals,
where we improvise our delight in secret corners. There are
    rivals
here or dear friends from towns where the red watermelons
    grow.

These urinals are where my friends dwell…Perhaps
I am not drawn to the mountains where one finds
(far from the sea and the perverse odors)
other adolescents who smell of figs?

The milkmaid quickly climbs down the steps,
and begins her work on the threshing floor. In the darkness
    of the barn
he feels a cluster grow in his pants. He is half asleep and
    dreaming.
Through an aperture, the pink light of early dawn falls
on the faces of the drowsy laborers. He feels the warm
    dewdrops
and the milky residue. His thoughts were not of her at all.

Unmoved and lost.

But something slowly animates the dark

and I can see a small hand emerging.

Alone and unable to sleep.
Now that the train has stopped,
he waits for a moment to catch his breath.
He hears the sigh of Italy in the night.
It is brief and yet, somehow,
it agrees with us…

The incessant summer rains oppress the city.
In the village, near the orchid there is a filthy boy
that dreamily guards his raised penis. Then he sighs
and again takes hold of his poet. And the hour descends.

There were many friends who shared
the same secret. Only one
never speaks about himself.

As much as I adore you,
the fundamental Nature in you that draws me to you,
imprisons me.

(She is calmly reading a book or looking out at the sea
for a long time. She is Mistress of the high tower.)

In the absence of sky and sea,
she proved false to me in the afternoon, and I knew
that my prison was her freedom.

Does beauty still exist in this brave new world?
I am not speaking of the thin, worn out faces of the workers.
At the train stations you see them, drunk at the end of the
    day.
O youth with your blazing eyes that gaze upon distant
    shores, alone.

It is sweet to cry when the sky is serene
and the water luminescent.
O juvenile despair.

The vacant nights are full of the sound of drum-beats
near the tracks. But under the silent moon
there is the cry of a heart beating.

TO RENZO VEPIGNANI

The nights descended slowly upon the city
and the world was blessed with peace.
My youth was delicate
like the gentle and unexpected joy of a soldier.

Then came the war and in our life
the nights were no longer patient and slow.
The sunsets were dull because of all the dust and smoke.
And the heavy malaise
that overcame us when Spring returned, was without end.

## TO EUGENIO MONTALE

I walk toward the festivals at dusk,
opposite the crowd who happily and quickly
rise from the stadium seats to cheer.
I don't look at anyone but I see everyone.
Sometimes I pick up a smile.
More rarely a familiar regard.

But I no longer remember who they are.
I know death solves nothing.
It is too unfair.
Even if I no longer remember who they are.

PETER VALENTE was born in Salerno, Italy and grew up in New Jersey. He holds a B.S. in Electrical Engineering from Stevens Institute of Technology. He is the author of the chapbook, *Forge of Words a Forest* (Jensen Daniels, 1998), and his poems have appeared in journals such as *Mirage #4/ Periodical, First Intensity, Prosodia, Aufgabe,* and *Talisman.* In the late 1990s, he co-edited the poetry magazines *Vapor/ Strains* and *Lady Blizzard's Batmobile* and wrote articles on jazz for the *Edgewater Reporter.* In 2010, he turned to filmmaking and has completed 60 shorts to date, 24 of which were screened at Anthology Film Archives. He has translated the work of Luis Cernuda, Nanni Balestrini and Pier Paolo Pasolini and is the co-translator of the chapbook, *Selected Late Letters of Antonin Artaud,* 1945-1947 (Portable Press at Yo-Yo Labs, 2014). His book, *The Artaud Variations,* is forthcoming from Spuyten Duyvil.

Lightning Source UK Ltd.
Milton Keynes UK
UKHW022059270921
391272UK00011B/2583

9 780692 296936